HOUGHTON MIFFLIN HARCOURT

WRITE SOURCE

D0861579

Assessment

Grade 3

Pretest
Progress Tests
Post-test

GREAT
SOURCE.

 HOUGHTON MIFFLIN HARCOURT

Contents

Assessments

Assessment and Instruction

In past decades, writing assessment was generally held to be the province of the teacher. Students turned in work—then waited to see what grades they would receive. Now it is widely recognized that learning to be a good assessor is one of the best ways to become a strong writer. In order to assess well, students must learn to recognize good writing. They must know and be able to describe the difference between writing that works and writing that does not work. Students learn to assess, generally, by going through three key steps:

- learning about the traits of writing by which their work—and that of others—will be assessed
- applying the traits to a wide variety of written texts
- applying the traits to their own work—first assessing it for strengths and weaknesses, then revising it as needed

Why should students be assessors?

Students who learn to be assessors also

- learn to think like professional writers
- take responsibility for their own revising
- make meaningful changes in their writing—instead of simply recopying a draft to make it look neater

Roles of Teachers and Students

Here is a quick summary of the kinds of activities teachers and students usually engage in while acting as assessors in the classroom.

Teachers

As assessors, teachers often engage in the following activities:

- roving conferences: roaming the classroom, observing students' work, and offering comments or questions that will help take students to the next step
- one-on-one conferences, in which students are asked to come prepared with a question they need answered
- informal comments—written or oral—in which the teacher offers a personal response or poses a reader's question
- reading student work, using a checklist
- tracking scores over time to calculate a final grade for a grading period

Students

As assessors, students often engage in the following activities:

- using rubrics (holistic and analytic)
- using assessment checklists
- assessing and discussing written work that the teacher shares with the class
- assessing their own work, using a rubric
- compiling a portfolio and reflecting on the written work included

Effective Assessment in the Classroom

Good assessment gives students a sense of how they are growing as writers. It indicates to teachers which students are finding success, as well as the kinds of help other students may need. To ensure that assessment is working in your classroom, here are some things you can do.

- Make sure ALL students know the criteria you will use to assess their writing. If you are going to use a rating sheet or rubric, provide them with copies.
- Give copies of rubrics or checklists to parents, too, so they can help their children know what is expected of them.
- Make sure your instruction and assessment match.
- Involve students regularly in assessing published work from a variety of sources, as well as in evaluating samples of your writing (either unfinished drafts or completed pieces) and in assessing their own work.
- Don't grade *everything* students write. Instead, encourage students to write *often;* then choose or have students choose a few pieces to grade.
- Respond to the content *first.* Then look at the conventions. Correctness is important, but if you comment on spelling and mechanics before content, the message to students is, "I don't care as much about what you say as I do about whether you spell everything correctly."
- Encourage students to save rough drafts and to collect pieces of work regularly in a portfolio. This type of collection gives students a broad picture of how they are progressing as writers.
- Ask students if they mind having comments written directly on their work. For some students, comments on sticky notes may seem less obtrusive.

Approaches for Assessing Writing (Summative)

The most common forms of direct writing assessment are listed below.

Analytical assessment identifies the features, or traits, that characterize effective writing, and defines them along a continuum of performance from *incomplete* (the first or lowest level) through *fair* (the middle level) to *excellent* (the highest level). Many analytical scales run from a low of 1 point to a high of 5 or 6 points. This form of assessment tells students exactly where their strengths and weaknesses lie: "Your writing has strong ideas but needs work on voice," or "Your writing has powerful voice but lacks accuracy."

Holistic assessment focuses on a piece of writing as a whole. In this sense, it is like letter grading. Holistic assessors often use a checklist of traits to identify the kinds of characteristics they're looking for; this is called focused holistic assessment. The assessors do not, however, score traits separately, so student writers do not know where they were most or least successful in their work.

Mode-specific assessment is similar to analytical assessment except that the rating scales or scoring guides (rubrics) are designed specifically for particular modes of writing, such as narrative, expository, persuasive, and so on. This kind of assessment works best in a structured curriculum where students will be assigned particular forms and subjects for writing.

Portfolio assessment gives students a chance to showcase their best writing or to document their growth as writers over time. In assembling a portfolio, students generally choose which pieces of writing they will complete and which ones they will include in their portfolios. (See pages 38–41 in the Student Edition.)

Assessment in *Write Source*

Using Rubrics Assessment of writing in *Write Source* is based on mode-specific rubrics. In each core unit—narrative, expository, and persuasive—genre-specific rubrics guide both the development of written work and the evaluation of the work. The rubrics are organized around the six traits of effective writing: ideas, organization, voice, word choice, sentence fluency, and conventions. Each trait is evaluated individually as part of a total assessment. When you first start using rubrics in the classroom, either with students' own work or with published writing, it may be more manageable to have students focus on one specific trait (such as organization). Gradually, you can add other traits until you ask students to evaluate a piece of writing for all of the traits.

Benchmark Papers In each core unit of the Student Edition—narrative, expository, and persuasive—you and your students have the opportunity to evaluate a student paper and review the self-assessment of that paper. This evaluation follows in-depth instruction on the genre. In addition, the Teacher's Edition provides a variety of copy masters for further assessment practice:

- Two additional Benchmark Papers that you can use with students represent different levels of expertise.
- A blank Assessment Sheet based on the traits of writing allows you and your students to rate the Benchmark Papers.
- A completed Assessment Sheet for each Benchmark Paper guides you and your students through evaluating the paper.

Following are the Benchmark Papers and their levels of competence.

Narrative Writing	**Persuasive Writing**
"Dancing Drums" *(strong)*	"Save Our Recess" *(strong)*
"The Snow Day" *(good)*	"New Sidewalks" *(good)*
"Looking for midnight" *(fair)*	"A New Pool" *(fair)*
Expository Writing	
"Learning by Doing and Going" *(strong)*	
"How to Bake a Cake" *(good)*	
"A Kite" *(fair)*	

Assessment Book In addition to rubric-based assessment of students' writing, teachers can assess students' writing with the four tests in this booklet.

The **Pretest** is designed to be administered at the beginning of the school year. It can help you determine your students' levels of writing experience and knowledge and what you might need to emphasize in your teaching. The Pretest also provides a baseline for measuring students' progress from the beginning of the year to the end.

Progress Test 1 and **Progress Test 2** may be administered at regular intervals during the year. These tests can help you monitor students' progress and refine your teaching plans as the school year proceeds.

© Houghton Mifflin Harcourt Publishing Company

The **Post-test** should be administered at the end of the year to help determine how much progress students have made.

Each Assessment Book test has three parts. *Part 1: Basic Elements of Writing* and *Part 2: Proofreading and Editing* comprise a total of 24 multiple-choice questions. Students choose the best answer to each question. Parts 1 and 2 of each test are aligned with two reference sections in the back of the Student Edition, "Basic Grammar and Writing" and "Proofreader's Guide." *Part 3: Writing* provides a writing prompt. Students respond by writing a paragraph.

Assessment and the Common Core Standards

In 2009, the Council of Chief State School Officers (CCSSO) and the National Governors Association (NGA) led the development of the Career and College Readiness Standards in reading, writing, speaking and listening, and mathematics. As a downward extension of this initiative, the Standards for Language Arts K–12 were developed in 2010. These standards describe the language arts skills and understandings that all students must learn in order to achieve career and college readiness.

The English Language Arts K–12 Common Core Standards divide the language arts into reading, writing, speaking and listening, and language development strands that comprise an integrated core curriculum. The writing skills are divided into those important to many types of writing and those that belong to specific modes such as narrative writing, informative/explanatory writing, and argument. The conventions standards in the language development strand include grammar and usage, mechanics, and the fundamentals of writing, as well as word choice and style.

Write Source provides rigorous yet motivating instruction in the English Language Arts K–12 Common Core Standards. Because this Assessment Book closely aligns to the *Write Source* instruction, it enables teachers to make sound instructional decisions for each student.

Administering the Tests

To administer a test, make a copy of the test pages for each student. Have students write their name and the date at the top of each page. Then read aloud the directions for each part of the test and make sure students understand what they are expected to do. For Parts 1 and 2, have students mark their answers on the test pages by choosing the best answer to each question and filling in the bubble beside the answer they choose. For Part 3, have students plan and write their paragraph on the test page or allow them to use separate paper.

Scoring the Tests

If you wish to keep a record of students' scores and/or track performance over time, begin by making a copy of the **Student Scoring Chart** (on page 10) for each student. To score each test, refer to the **Answer Key** for the test (on page 11) to check each student's answers. Circle the number of each item answered correctly. Then count the total number correct and write it in the *# Correct* column of the chart (see example on the following page).

Parts 1 and 2: Calculating Percent Scores

To find a Percent Score (for Part 1, Part 2, or Parts 1 and 2 combined), divide the number correct by the number of items. For example:

Part 1 has 16 items. A student who answers 12 items correctly has a score of 12/16; $12 \div 16 = 0.75$, or 75%.

Part 2 has 8 items. A student who answers 4 items correctly has a score of 4/8; $4 \div 8 = 0.5$, or 50%.

The total number of multiple-choice items in Parts 1 and 2 combined is 24. A student who answers a combined total of 16 items correctly has a score of 16/24; $16 \div 24 = 0.667$, or about 67%.

Record the percent scores in the *Pct Score* column of the scoring chart. You may use this chart to record and compare a student's scores on all four tests during the year.

Pretest	# Correct	Pct Score
Part 1: Basic Elements of Writing 1 2 3 4 5 6 7 8 9 10 11 12 13 14 15 16	_12_ / 16	= _75_ %
Part 2: Proofreading and Editing 17 18 19 20 21 22 23 24	_4_ / 8	= _50_ %
TOTAL (multiple-choice)	_16_ / 24	= _67_ %
Part 3: Writing	Overall Score:	

Part 3

To score Part 3 of the test, use the 6-point scoring rubric provided in the *Write Source* Student Edition or Teacher's Edition for narrative writing (pages 108–109) or expository writing (pages 160–161). Rate the student's writing on each of the six traits and calculate the average rating to obtain an overall score between 0 and 6. Alternatively, a 4-point and a 5-point rubric can be found in the Copy Masters section of the Teacher's Edition.

To pass a test, students should score at least 70% correct on the multiple-choice items (Parts 1 and 2 combined) and at least 3 out of 6 on the written paragraph. For any student who scores 70% or lower, you may want to analyze the student's test responses more closely. Use the **Tested Skills Chart** on page 9 of this book to find the skill or content tested by each item. By checking to see which items a student answered incorrectly, you can identify areas for further instruction.

© Houghton Mifflin Harcourt Publishing Company

Tested Skills

SUBTEST/Tested Skills	Pretest	Progress Test 1	Progress Test 2	Post-test
PART 1: BASIC ELEMENTS OF WRITING				
Words				
Using nouns (singular/plural, common/proper)	7	10	10	6
Using possessive pronouns	3	8	1	7
Using verbs (past, present, future)	8, 9	1, 6	8, 9	5, 8
Using adjectives and adverbs	5, 6	3, 4	4, 6	1, 9
Using prepositions and prepositional phrases	1	5	3	10
Using coordinating conjunctions	10	7	2	2
Sentences				
Complete sentences, run-ons, and fragments	11, 14	11, 14	11, 14	11, 13
Subject-verb agreement	2, 4	2, 9	5, 7	3, 4
Sentence style	12, 13	12, 13	12, 13	12, 14
Paragraphs				
Types of paragraphs	15	15	15	15
Topic sentences, details, and organization	16	16	16	16
PART 2: PROOFREADING AND EDITING				
End punctuation	22	24	22	23
Commas in series and dates	21	22	23	21
Apostrophes in contractions and possessives	20	23	24	20
Quotation marks	24	21	20	19
Capitalization	17	17	17	22
Spelling	18	20	21	17
Using the right word	19	19	18	18
Using the parts of speech	23	18	19	24
PART 3: WRITING				
Writing a narrative paragraph	✓			✓
Writing an expository paragraph		✓	✓	

Student Scoring Chart

Student Name _____   Grade _____

Teacher Name _____   Class _____

Pretest	# Correct	Pct Score
Part 1: Basic Elements of Writing 1 2 3 4 5 6 7 8 9 10 11 12 13 14 15 16	_____ / 16	= _____ %
Part 2: Proofreading and Editing 17 18 19 20 21 22 23 24	_____ / 8	= _____ %
TOTAL (multiple-choice)	_____ / 24	= _____ %
Part 3: Writing	Overall Score:	

Progress Test 1	# Correct	Pct Score
Part 1: Basic Elements of Writing 1 2 3 4 5 6 7 8 9 10 11 12 13 14 15 16	_____ / 16	= _____ %
Part 2: Proofreading and Editing 17 18 19 20 21 22 23 24	_____ / 8	= _____ %
TOTAL (multiple-choice)	_____ / 24	= _____ %
Part 3: Writing	Overall Score:	

Progress Test 2	# Correct	Pct Score
Part 1: Basic Elements of Writing 1 2 3 4 5 6 7 8 9 10 11 12 13 14 15 16	_____ / 16	= _____ %
Part 2: Proofreading and Editing 17 18 19 20 21 22 23 24	_____ / 8	= _____ %
TOTAL (multiple-choice)	_____ / 24	= _____ %
Part 3: Writing	Overall Score:	

Post-test	# Correct	Pct Score
Part 1: Basic Elements of Writing 1 2 3 4 5 6 7 8 9 10 11 12 13 14 15 16	_____ / 16	= _____ %
Part 2: Proofreading and Editing 17 18 19 20 21 22 23 24	_____ / 8	= _____ %
TOTAL (multiple-choice)	_____ / 24	= _____ %
Part 3: Writing	Overall Score:	

© Houghton Mifflin Harcourt Publishing Company

Answer Keys

Pretest *pp. 14–19*

Part 1: Basic Elements of Writing

1. c	5. b	9. b	13. d
2. b	6. d	10. c	14. b
3. d	7. a	11. a	15. a
4. a	8. c	12. c	16. d

Part 2: Proofreading and Editing

17. b	19. a	21. b	23. c
18. d	20. a	22. d	24. a

Part 3: Writing

(See Rubric for Narrative Writing on pp. 108–109 of *Write Source* Student Edition or Teacher's Edition)

Progress Test 2 *pp. 30–36*

Part 1: Basic Elements of Writing

1. a	5. b	9. a	13. c
2. c	6. d	10. d	14. b
3. b	7. a	11. b	15. c
4. c	8. d	12. a	16. a

Part 2: Proofreading and Editing

17. a	19. b	21. b	23. c
18. c	20. a	22. a	24. c

Part 3: Writing

(See Rubric for Expository Writing on pp. 160–161 of *Write Source* Student Edition or Teacher's Edition)

Progress Test 1 *pp. 22–27*

Part 1: Basic Elements of Writing

1. b	5. a	9. a	13. a
2. c	6. a	10. c	14. d
3. c	7. b	11. a	15. c
4. d	8. b	12. d	16. d

Part 2: Proofreading and Editing

17. a	19. a	21. c	23. a
18. c	20. d	22. d	24. b

Part 3: Writing

(See Rubric for Expository Writing on pp. 160–161 of *Write Source* Student Edition or Teacher's Edition)

Post-test *pp. 38–43*

Part 1: Basic Elements of Writing

1. b	5. d	9. a	13. b
2. c	6. c	10. c	14. d
3. a	7. b	11. d	15. a
4. b	8. c	12. c	16. c

Part 2: Proofreading and Editing

17. c	19. c	21. d	23. a
18. a	20. d	22. b	24. c

Part 3: Writing

(See Rubric for Narrative Writing on pp. 108–109 of *Write Source* Student Edition or Teacher's Edition)

Pretest

Pretest

Part 1: Basic Elements of Writing

Questions 1–10: Read each sentence and look at the underlined part. It may have a mistake in the way it is written. Choose the best way to write the underlined part of the sentence. If there is no mistake, choose answer **d,** "Correct as it is."

1 Some birds fly south <u>on</u> the winter.
   (a) at
   (b) into
   (c) for
   (d) Correct as it is

2 Other birds <u>stays</u> in the same place all year.
   (a) staying
   (b) stay
   (c) stayed
   (d) Correct as it is

3 Two bluebirds made a nest for <u>their</u> eggs.
   (a) it's
   (b) theirs
   (c) its
   (d) Correct as it is

4 That bird <u>have</u> a nest under the deck.
   (a) has
   (b) haves
   (c) having
   (d) Correct as it is

5 A dead tree is a <u>best</u> place for a nest.
   (a) more better
   (b) good
   (c) goodest
   (d) Correct as it is

6 Two birds working together can make a nest <u>quickly</u>.
   (a) quick
   (b) quickest
   (c) more quicker
   (d) Correct as it is

7 The Robin has light blue eggs.

   ⓐ robin

   ⓑ Robins

   ⓒ robins

   ⓓ Correct as it is

8 Last spring, a bird builded a nest on our porch.

   ⓐ is building

   ⓑ build

   ⓒ built

   ⓓ Correct as it is

9 We did seen many birds at our house this year.

   ⓐ are seen

   ⓑ have seen

   ⓒ has saw

   ⓓ Correct as it is

10 Many baby birds eat worms, or some eat only insects.

   ⓐ so

   ⓑ if

   ⓒ but

   ⓓ Correct as it is

Questions 11–14: Read each question and choose the best answer.

11 Which is a complete sentence written correctly?

   ⓐ Dad gave us some coins to count.

   ⓑ Always has change jingling in his pockets!

   ⓒ My dad, my little brother, and me.

   ⓓ Have enough coins for the bus?

12 Which is the best way to combine these two sentences?

> I collect quarters.
> The quarters come from different states.

   ⓐ I collect quarters, and they come from different states.

   ⓑ I collect quarters, the quarters from different states.

   ⓒ I collect quarters from different states.

   ⓓ I collect quarters and come from different states.

13 Which is an exclamatory sentence that should end with an exclamation point?

- (a) Make a different pile for each coin
- (b) How much do all these coins weigh
- (c) I wonder how much these nickels weigh
- (d) I can't believe how heavy these coins are

14 Which is a run-on sentence that should be written as two sentences?

- (a) Each state quarter looks different from the other state quarters.
- (b) Georgia's quarter has a peach Iowa's quarter has a schoolhouse.
- (c) Many of the designs show important events in a state's history.
- (d) California's quarter has an important person on it.

Questions 15–16: A student wrote this paragraph about a trip. It may need some changes or corrections. Read the paragraph. Then choose the best answer to each question.

My Big Move

(1) When I was 5 years old, my family moved from Ohio to Colorado. (2) The first day of driving was exciting. (3) On the second day, we crossed the Mississippi River. (4) Now we were really in the West! (5) Then I slept a lot because everything was so flat. (6) Our car climbed and climbed. (7) Finally, we saw mountains. (8) That night I saw more stars than I'd ever seen before. (9) It was sad to leave Ohio, but our new home state is really beautiful.

---

15 What type of paragraph is this?

- (a) narrative
- (b) persuasive
- (c) expository
- (d) response to literature

16 Which two sentences should be switched to organize the paragraph better?

- (a) sentences 3 and 4
- (b) sentences 4 and 5
- (c) sentences 5 and 6
- (d) sentences 6 and 7

Part 2: Proofreading and Editing

Questions 17–24: Read the passage and the letter. Look carefully at the underlined parts. They may have mistakes in capitalization, punctuation, spelling, or word usage. Choose the best way to write each underlined part.

My favorite place is <u>lake evergreen</u> near my house. My <u>friends</u> and
                     17   **18**

I <u>meat</u> there almost every day. We ride our bikes or float paper boats in
 19

the water. Sometimes we get ice cream. Near the lake is the train station.

Late in the afternoon, I go there and wait for my <u>dads'</u> train. Then we
                                            20

walk home together.

17
  (a) lake Evergreen
  (b) Lake Evergreen
  (c) "lake evergreen"
  (d) Best as it is

18
  (a) frenz
  (b) frends
  (c) freinds
  (d) Best as it is

19
  (a) meet
  (b) mete
  (c) mat
  (d) Best as it is

20
  (a) dad's
  (b) dads's
  (c) dads
  (d) Best as it is

August 23 2012,
21

Dear Terrell,

We're having a great time in Boston! Yesterday we went on a
22

whale watch. Today we walked on the Freedom Trail, watched jugglers,

and ate fried clams. Tomorrow me and my uncle are going to Truro
23

Beach. He said, It's the best beach in the world! I can't wait to swim in
24

the ocean! You would love it here.

Your buddy,

Ramon

21 (a) August, 23, 2012
    (b) August 23, 2012
    (c) August 23 2012
    (d) Best as it is

22 (a) Boston:
    (b) Boston?
    (c) Boston,
    (d) Best as it is

23 (a) me and my Uncle
    (b) my uncle and me
    (c) my uncle and I
    (d) Best as it is

24 (a) "It's the best beach in the world!"
    (b) 'It's the best beach in the world!'
    (c) (It's the best beach in the world!)
    (d) Best as it is

Part 3: Writing

Choose one day that you really enjoyed. It might have been a day in school or a vacation day. Write a narrative paragraph telling what you did that day.

You may want to jot down some ideas or use a graphic organizer to help plan your narrative. Remember that a narrative tells a story about something that has happened. It should have a clear beginning, middle, and ending.

_____

_____

_____

_____

_____

_____

_____

_____

_____

_____

_____

_____

_____

_____

_____

_____

_____

_____

Progress Test 1

Name _____ Date _____

Progress Test 1

Part 1: Basic Elements of Writing

Questions 1–10: Read each sentence and look at the underlined part. It may have a mistake in the way it is written. Choose the best way to write the underlined part of the sentence. If there is no mistake, choose answer **d,** "Correct as it is."

1 Every day after school, Rosa <u>playing</u> kickball.
   (a) play
   (b) plays
   (c) is played
   (d) Correct as it is

2 Rosa and her friends <u>loves</u> to play together.
   (a) loving
   (b) is loved
   (c) love
   (d) Correct as it is

3 She is the <u>faster</u> runner in third grade.
   (a) fast
   (b) most fast
   (c) fastest
   (d) Correct as it is

4 Rosa's team <u>usually</u> wins the game.
   (a) most usual
   (b) usual
   (c) usualler
   (d) Correct as it is

5 Everyone wants to be <u>along her team</u> because she's so good.
   (a) on her team
   (b) near her team
   (c) for her team
   (d) Correct as it is

6 Suddenly, a new boy <u>shown</u> up.
   (a) shows
   (b) show
   (c) showing
   (d) Correct as it is

7 Omar's not very tall, <u>so</u> he can really kick the ball.
ⓐ and
ⓑ but
ⓒ if
ⓓ Correct as it is

8 They all want to be on <u>he's</u> team now.
ⓐ they're
ⓑ his
ⓒ his'
ⓓ Correct as it is

9 Kickball games <u>is</u> really fun.
ⓐ are
ⓑ was
ⓒ being
ⓓ Correct as it is

10 The <u>child</u> cheer loudly.
ⓐ Child
ⓑ childs
ⓒ children
ⓓ Correct as it is

Questions 11–14: Read each question and choose the best answer.

11 Which is a complete sentence written correctly?
ⓐ The Mexican flag is green, white, and red.
ⓑ The peaceful rule of the Mayas.
ⓒ After Mayan rule ended in the 1500s.
ⓓ Ride donkeys through the mountains.

12 Which is the best way to combine these two sentences?

> Mexican farmers grow squash and corn.
> Mexican farmers grow beans, too.

ⓐ Mexican farmers grow squash and corn, and they grow beans, too.
ⓑ Mexican farmers grow squash and corn, and beans, too.
ⓒ Squash and corn and beans are grown by Mexican farmers.
ⓓ Mexican farmers grow squash, corn, and beans.

13 Which is an interrogative sentence that should end with a question mark?

ⓐ Which crops are grown together

ⓑ How green those plants are

ⓒ The beans climb up the corn plants

ⓓ Squash leaves give shade for the roots

14 Which is a run-on sentence that should be written as two sentences?

ⓐ People learned to grow corn there 6,000 years ago.

ⓑ Spanish explorers brought horses to Mexico.

ⓒ The Mayan people had calendars 1,500 years ago.

ⓓ No one knows why the Mayas left their cities it may have been sickness.

Questions 15–16: A student wrote this paragraph about doing laundry. It may need some changes or corrections. Read the paragraph. Then choose the best answer to each question.

Doing Laundry

(1) Doing laundry is easy. (2) First, sort the clothes into colors and whites. (3) Then take out everything that should be washed by hand. (4) Measure soap into the washing machine. (5) Choose the cycle. (6) Press the start button. (7) When the wash is done, hang the clothes outside. (8) The only part I don't like is putting the socks together.

---

15 What type of paragraph is this?

ⓐ descriptive

ⓑ response to literature

ⓒ expository

ⓓ narrative

16 Which sentence should be removed to improve the paragraph?

ⓐ sentence 5

ⓑ sentence 6

ⓒ sentence 7

ⓓ sentence 8

Part 2: Proofreading and Editing

Questions 17–24: Read the passage and the letter. Look carefully at the underlined parts. They may have mistakes in capitalization, punctuation, spelling, or word usage. Choose the best way to write each underlined part.

> Northern Canada is a very cold place. When I think of Northern
>
> Canada, I think of the <u>ice age</u>! For at least 10,000 years, the Inuit people
>   **17**
>
> have lived, hunted, and fished there. Some live in igloos made of ice and
>
> snow. In the summer, <u>them</u> hunt for seals and whales. Some people carve
>   **18**
>
> wooden eagles, <u>witch</u> help to <u>protect</u> them.
>   **19**   **20**

17
(a) Ice Age
(b) Ice age
(c) ice Age
(c) Best as it is

18
(a) him
(b) we
(c) they
(d) Best as it is

19
(a) which
(b) watch
(c) what
(d) Best as it is

20
(a) pratect
(b) pretect
(c) proteck
(d) Best as it is

November 10, 2012

Dear Aunt Tiana,

Thank you so much for my birthday party. My friend Ron

said, <u>It was awesome!</u> The <u>food, music, and decorations</u> were great!
    21   **22**

Thanks for the movie passes, too. <u>We'are</u> going to the movies on Thursday.
                             23

You are <u>the best aunt,</u>
          24

                    Love,

                    Hannah

21
  (a) (It was awesome!)
  (b) 'It was awesome!'
  (c) "It was awesome!"
  (d) Best as it is

22
  (a) food, music, and decorations,
  (b) food and music and decorations
  (c) food music and decorations
  (d) Best as it is

23
  (a) We're
  (b) We re
  (c) We-re
  (d) Best as it is

24
  (a) the best aunt?
  (b) the best aunt!
  (c) the best aunt—
  (d) Best as it is

Part 3: Writing

How do you get to school each day? You may walk, get a ride in a car, or take a bus. Write an expository paragraph explaining how you get to school each day. Tell the route that you take from your home to the school.

You may want to jot down some ideas or use a graphic organizer to help plan your explanation. Remember that an expository paragraph should include a topic sentence and supporting details.

_____

_____

_____

_____

_____

_____

_____

_____

_____

_____

_____

_____

_____

_____

_____

_____

_____

_____

Progress Test 2

Progress Test 2

Part 1: Basic Elements of Writing

Questions 1–10: Read each sentence and look at the underlined part. It may have a mistake in the way it is written. Choose the best way to write the underlined part of the sentence. If there is no mistake, choose answer **d,** "Correct as it is."

1 Mr. Cross and his son sell lobsters at <u>they</u> store.
  ⓐ their
  ⓑ they're
  ⓒ them
  ⓓ Correct as it is

2 A lobster has a hard shell <u>but</u> two eyes.
  ⓐ also
  ⓑ or
  ⓒ and
  ⓓ Correct as it is

3 Mr. Cross steered his boat <u>on the rock.</u>
  ⓐ over the rock.
  ⓑ around the rock.
  ⓒ through the rock.
  ⓓ Correct as it is

4 Lobsters move <u>slow</u> along the sea bottom.
  ⓐ slowing
  ⓑ slowed
  ⓒ slowly
  ⓓ Correct as it is

5 Boiling <u>are</u> the best way to cook crabs and lobsters.
  ⓐ be
  ⓑ is
  ⓒ were
  ⓓ Correct as it is

6 Lobsters from Maine are <u>larger</u> than lobsters from Florida.
  ⓐ large
  ⓑ largely
  ⓒ largest
  ⓓ Correct as it is

7 In New England, people <u>uses</u> traps to catch crabs.

    (a) use

    (b) using

    (c) is using

    (d) Correct as it is

8 Crabs that are too small must be <u>thrown</u> back.

    (a) throwed

    (b) threw

    (c) throw

    (d) Correct as it is

9 How many crabs did you <u>catched</u> today?

    (a) catch

    (b) catches

    (c) caught

    (d) Correct as it is

10 The restaurant called <u>Marley's Fishing Dock</u> is always busy.

    (a) marley's fishing dock

    (b) Marley's fishing dock

    (c) Marley's fishing Dock

    (d) Correct as it is

Questions 11–14: Read each question and choose the best answer.

11 Which is a complete sentence written correctly?

    (a) Claudia, my aunt.

    (b) She is going to marry Brandon.

    (c) Are getting married in a church.

    (d) Will go to my cousin's house afterward.

12 Which is an exclamatory sentence that should end with an exclamation point?

    (a) What a huge cake

    (b) Where does he come from

    (c) I wonder when they'll cut the cake

    (d) It's a little noisy in here

Progress Test 2

13 Which is the best way to combine these two sentences?

> Grandpa danced at the wedding.
> Grandpa sang at the wedding, too.

ⓐ Grandpa danced at the wedding and sang, too.

ⓑ Grandpa danced and sang at the wedding, too.

ⓒ Grandpa danced and sang at the wedding.

ⓓ Grandpa danced at the wedding, and Grandpa sang.

14 Which is a run-on sentence that should be written as two sentences?

ⓐ The band began to play as soon as we got to the hall.

ⓑ Dinner was served at 6:00 the band began playing at 8:00.

ⓒ My cousins Leandro and Daniel had never danced a waltz before.

ⓓ Uncle Sal is dancing with Julie's grandmother.

Questions 15–16: A student wrote this paragraph about the Cherokee people. It may need some changes or corrections. Read the paragraph. Then choose the best answer to each question.

> (1) Many Cherokee people now live in Oklahoma, but they did not always live there. (2) Once they lived in western Georgia. (3) They had roads, schools, and churches. (4) In 1838, the Cherokee were forced to leave their native lands. (5) They had to travel far to the west. (6) Their journey became known as the "Trail of Tears."

15 What type of paragraph is this?

ⓐ narrative

ⓑ response to literature

ⓒ expository

ⓓ persuasive

16 Which detail sentence could best be added between sentences 5 and 6?

ⓐ About 4,000 Cherokee died along the way.

ⓑ Georgia is located on the Atlantic Ocean.

ⓒ Utah and Wyoming are two Western states.

ⓓ Many people left Oklahoma in the 1930s.

Part 2: Proofreading and Editing

Questions 17–24: Read the passage and the letter. Look carefully at the underlined parts. They may have mistakes in capitalization, punctuation, spelling, or word usage. Choose the best way to write each underlined part.

Making Compost

Compost is good "food" for your garden. My dad and I make compost at

our home in <u>austin, Texas</u>. Making compost is simple. Start with a pile of dry

　　　　　　17

leaves. Put them in a barrel with <u>wholes</u> in it. Add some vegetable scraps and

　　　　　　　　　　　　　　18

grass, and throw in a little dirt. Add more scraps, grass, and dirt each week

until the barrel is full. Pour some water on it every week. <u>Sooner,</u> you'll have

　　　　　　　　　　　　　　　　　　　　　　　　19

rich, black compost to feed your plants. My dad says, <u>Every gardener should</u>

　　　　　　　　　　　　　　　　　　　　　　　　20

<u>have a compost pile.</u>

17
(a) Austin, Texas
(b) austin, texas
(c) Austin, texas
(d) Best as it is

18
(a) whole
(b) halls
(c) holes
(d) Best as it is

19
(a) Soonest
(b) Soon
(c) Soonly
(d) Best as it is

20
(a) "Every gardener should have a compost pile."
(b) 'Every gardener should have a compost pile.'
(c) (Every gardener should have a compost pile.)
(d) Best as it is

August 23, 2012

Dear Mrs. Jackson,

   We are having a yard sale next <u>Saterday</u>. You are welcome to join the sale if
                                              21

you have anything to <u>sell?</u> We plan to offer all of these things: <u>pots pans, books toys</u>
                          22   **23**

<u>tools,</u> and furniture. If you are interested, bring your things to the <u>Clarks house</u> on
                                                                               24

Friday.

                                              Thank you,

                                              Matt Moran

21 (a) Satterday
   (b) Saturday
   (c) Satturday
   (d) Best as it is

22 (a) sell.
   (b) sell,
   (c) sell:
   (d) Best as it is

23 (a) pots and pans, and books, and toys, and tools,
   (b) pots and pans, books and toys, and tools,
   (c) pots, pans, books, toys, tools,
   (d) Best as it is

24 (a) Clark's house
   (b) Clarks house's
   (c) Clarks' house
   (d) Best as it is

Name _____ Date _____

Part 3: Writing

What is your favorite season? Write an expository paragraph explaining what your favorite season is and why. Give at least three reasons for your choice.

You may want to jot down some ideas or use a graphic organizer to help plan your explanation. Remember that an expository paragraph should include a topic sentence and supporting details.

_____
_____
_____
_____
_____
_____
_____
_____
_____
_____
_____
_____
_____
_____
_____
_____
_____
_____

Post-test

Post-test

Part 1: Basic Elements of Writing

Questions 1–10: Read each sentence and look at the underlined part. It may have a mistake in the way it is written. Choose the best way to write the underlined part of the sentence. If there is no mistake, choose answer **d**, "Correct as it is."

1 Raccoons are <u>smart</u> than most animals.

    ⓐ smartest

    ⓑ smarter

    ⓒ smartly

    ⓓ Correct as it is

2 A raccoon's tail has either four <u>and</u> five black rings.

    ⓐ but

    ⓑ also

    ⓒ or

    ⓓ Correct as it is

3 All raccoons <u>has</u> black masks over their faces.

    ⓐ have

    ⓑ is having

    ⓒ having

    ⓓ Correct as it is

4 They <u>uses</u> their paws like hands.

    ⓐ using

    ⓑ use

    ⓒ are used

    ⓓ Correct as it is

5 Raccoons <u>can open</u> jars with their paws.

    ⓐ can opening

    ⓑ can opened

    ⓒ are open

    ⓓ Correct as it is

6 A <u>raccoons</u> eats many different foods.

    ⓐ Raccoons

    ⓑ Raccoon

    ⓒ raccoon

    ⓓ Correct as it is

7 I borrowed <u>him</u> book about raccoons.

   ⓐ he's

   ⓑ his

   ⓒ he

   ⓓ Correct as it is

8 It <u>eated</u> some food from the garbage can.

   ⓐ eating

   ⓑ ated

   ⓒ ate

   ⓓ Correct as it is

9 Raccoons can see <u>very good</u> at night.

   ⓐ very well

   ⓑ much gooder

   ⓒ really good

   ⓓ Correct as it is

10 Do more raccoons live <u>off</u> the country or the city?

   ⓐ on

   ⓑ at

   ⓒ in

   ⓓ Correct as it is

Questions 11–14: Read each question and choose the best answer.

11 Which is a complete sentence written correctly?

   ⓐ Her head bending over her hands.

   ⓑ Sitting at a small table by the fire.

   ⓒ Blue, yellow, and purple beads everywhere.

   ⓓ Sharon is making a necklace.

12 Which is the best way to combine these two sentences?

> She uses strong thread.
> The thread is thin, too.

   ⓐ She uses strong thread that is also thin.

   ⓑ She uses strong thread and thin thread.

   ⓒ She uses strong, thin thread.

   ⓓ She uses strong thread and it's thin.

13 Which is a run-on sentence that should be written as two sentences?

ⓐ Some beads look like seeds, and others are long tubes.

ⓑ Some are copper balls some beads look like flowers.

ⓒ The purple glass beads are the prettiest.

ⓓ Beads come in many different shapes and sizes.

14 Which is an interrogative sentence that should end with a question mark?

ⓐ Those beads are made of glass

ⓑ What a beautiful necklace

ⓒ The blue and silver beads are pretty

ⓓ Whose necklace is that

Questions 15–16: A student wrote this paragraph about statues and acid rain. It may need some changes or corrections. Read the paragraph. Then choose the best answer to each question.

Why Old Statues Crumble

(1) Have you ever looked at old statues in parks? (2) Many statues are missing noses or fingers, or the shoulders slope. (3) These statues are made of limestone. (4) In the past 50 years, acid rain has become a real problem. (5) It can ruin a statue in a few years.

---

15 What type of paragraph is this?

ⓐ expository

ⓑ response to literature

ⓒ persuasive

ⓓ narrative

16 Where could this sentence best be added?

Limestone can be damaged by acid rain.

ⓐ between sentences 1 and 2

ⓑ between sentences 2 and 3

ⓒ between sentences 3 and 4

ⓓ between sentences 4 and 5

Part 2: Proofreading and Editing

Questions 17–24: Read the passage and the letter. Look carefully at the underlined parts. They may have mistakes in capitalization, punctuation, spelling, or word usage. Choose the best way to write each underlined part.

"May I ask a <u>cuestion</u>, Senator Philips?" said Younis very politely.
17

"Of course," the Senator said as he stood and <u>weighted</u> on the stage.
18

"Do you support keeping school open all year round?" Younis asked.

"Or do you think it should be closed for the summer?"

"Well, I can see why you'd want to know <u>that, the</u> Senator chuckled.
19

"<u>I'm</u> pleased to tell you that I think summer should always be a holiday!"
20

17
(a) kweschun
(b) queschion
(c) question
(d) Best as it is

18
(a) waited
(b) waitered
(c) weighed
(d) Best as it is

19
(a) that" the
(b) that the
(c) that," the
(d) Best as it is

20
(a) Im
(b) I'am
(c) Im'
(d) Best as it is

October 27, 2012
21

Dear <u>dr</u> Peabody,
22

I want to learn to read and speak the Japanese language. Your son

George says that you wrote a book about Japan, so I thought you might

be able to help. Where should I <u>start</u>. Do you know any teachers? Thank
23

you for any help you can <u>give I</u>.
24

Sincerely,

Anitra (George's friend)

21
  (a) October 27 2012
  (b) October, 27, 2012
  (c) October 27 2012,
  (d) Best as it is

22
  (a) DR.
  (b) Dr.
  (c) dr.
  (d) Best as it is

23
  (a) start?
  (b) start,
  (c) start!
  (d) Best as it is

24
  (a) give myself
  (b) give it
  (c) give me
  (d) Best as it is

Part 3: Writing

Think of something fun you have done with a parent or other family member. Write a narrative paragraph telling about what you did.

You may want to jot down some ideas or use a graphic organizer to help plan your narrative. Remember that a narrative tells a story about something that has happened. It should have a clear beginning, middle, and ending.

_____

_____

_____

_____

_____

_____

_____

_____

_____

_____

_____

_____

_____

_____

_____

_____

_____

Post-test